D1123734

Youme.
Mali under the night
sky : a Lao story of hom
c2010.
33305222450011
sa          02/24/11

# Mali Under the Night Sky

## A Lao Story of Home

written and illustrated by YOUME

When Mali was very young, she already
knew that the world was big—*ngai*—
and full of wonderful things.

She loved to sit in front of her house
and ask everyone,
"Where are you going—*jiao pai sai?*"

The people went everywhere!

ໄປງານບຸນ ··· to festivals,

ໄປເຮັດວຽກ ··· to work,

ໄປຕະຫລາດ

ໄປຢາມຄອບຄົວ ··· to visit family,

to play, ··· ໄປ ຫລິ້ນ

to the fields,

to market,

ไปนา

ไปลอยน้ำ

to swim,

ไปวัด

to the temple,

Where did Mali like to go?

Catching tiny fish in the rice field.
Quick, quick—*vai, vai!*

Finding pale
bamboo shoots in
the dark forest.
"Where are you
—*jiao yusai?*"

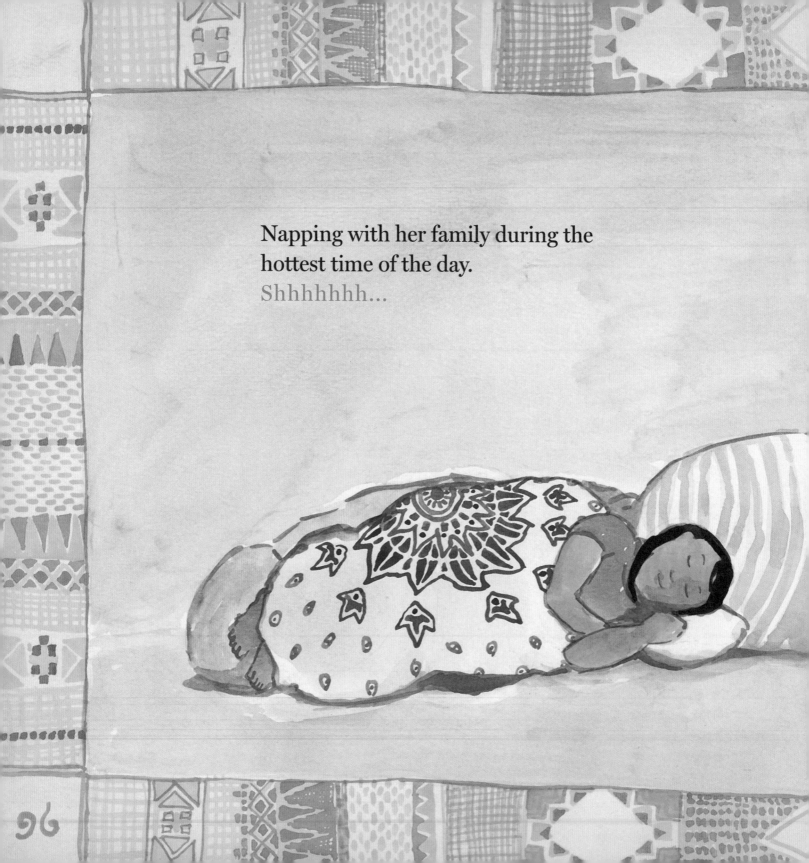

Napping with her family during the
hottest time of the day.
Shhhhhhh…

96

She loved to make feasts with
her aunts, spicy hot and
delicious—*saep lai!*

On very special days, for weddings, or when someone was traveling far away, family and friends gathered to eat, to dance together and to tie strings around each other's wrists.

This was a way of showing that their hearts would always be together—*soag sai, soag sai, soag sai.*

But something was changing where Mali lived. People stopped going everywhere. No one sat outside their houses to greet their friends. Fighting in neighboring countries was bringing danger to the land and the people. Even the birds were disappearing.

One night, the strings were for Mali and her family. Mali wondered— *Would she be leaving her home?*

That night, Mali listened to her parents, grandparents, aunts and uncles talking. "You have to take the children. No one is safe here. The war is getting closer."

Only a few hours later her family hurried
through the mysterious night. When they
saw soldiers on the road, they slipped
in behind the trees and did not make a
sound. A cloud covered the moon.
They came to the wide Mekong River.
How would they ever cross it?

24

Mali felt her father's strong arms lift her up and put her into a small wooden boat. The clouds passed away and the clear round moon shone high in the sky, reflecting on the water and the family quietly crossing.

Her mother offered rice, flowers
and prayers to the spirits of water,
asking that the family be safe and
comfortable—*sabai, sabai.*

สะบาย
สะบาย

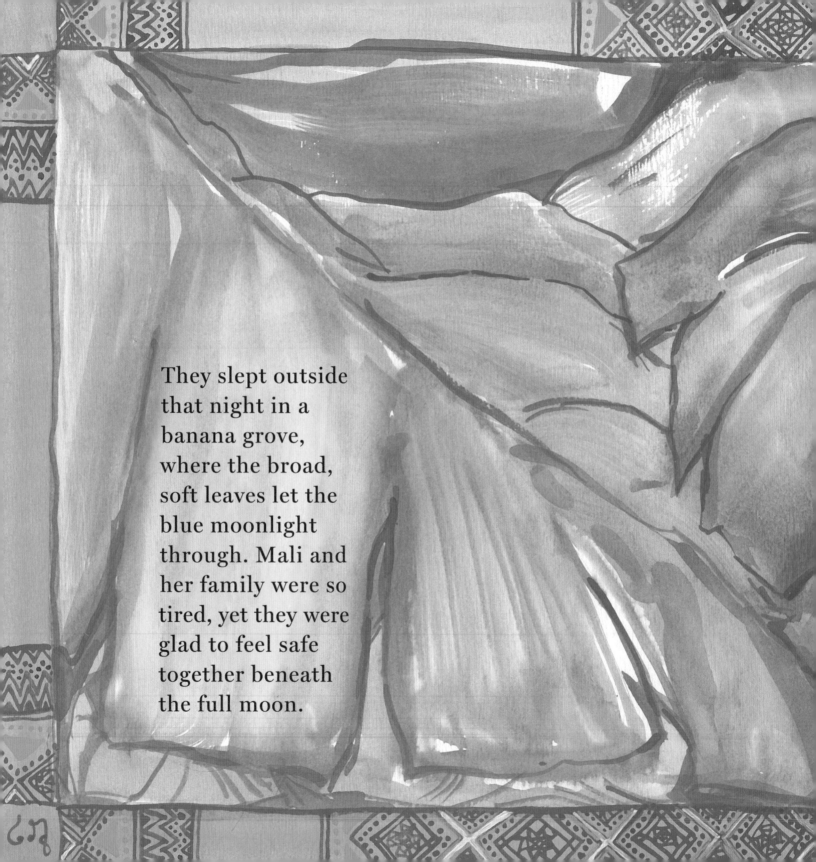

They slept outside that night in a banana grove, where the broad, soft leaves let the blue moonlight through. Mali and her family were so tired, yet they were glad to feel safe together beneath the full moon.

But the other side of the
river was a new country.
And when they woke up,
they found themselves
lost with so many other
traveling families. Men
came and arrested them
for not having a home.

Now Mali was in the
worst place she had ever
been, a crowded jail.
Angry tired jailers.
No flowers, no fish.
No trees and no home.

Was everything lost to her?

Mali looked at her wrists, and saw the strings that tied her to her beautiful home. She told everyone in the jail her memories. Everyone who heard her felt that they too were climbing trees, catching fish and feeling both free and loved. They remembered their own beautiful homes. And though the journey to a new home would be long and hard, their hearts were safe when they remembered where they had come from. *Soag sai*—blessings.

*Self Portrait*, Malichansouk Kouanchao, 2003, 32" x 48", mixed media. From the collection of the Family Housing Fund.

# I am Mali.

My full name is Malichansouk Kouanchao. *Mali* means jasmine flower and *chansouk* means full moon, but when you put my name together it also means "fortuitously guided by the lights of the night sky." I really lived the experiences in this book. I grew up to be an artist and an activist so that all people may celebrate their own creativity even in the most difficult situations.

I have lived in many different countries. Everywhere I meet artists (and there are as many ways to be an artist as there are people to meet) and when we share about where we have come from, we all find that our homes are safe in our hearts, even though they may not have been safe in the world, and the home that we share with one another is a brighter place for everyone's part in it.

## Healing the Wounds of War
### by Thavisouk Phrasavath
*As told to Jessica Powers*

Laos is a country surrounded by other countries, sharing its borders with Myanmar (Burma) and China to the northwest, Vietnam to the east, Cambodia to the south and Thailand to the west. I was born in 1964 in Laos during the civil war. There has never been a time without war for me.

I first realized I was in the middle of the war in a single moment. It was afternoon. The city was quiet. There was a bomb explosion. I looked up at the sky and I saw a rocket coming. All of a sudden, I saw someone blown away. Like dust, like one breath of life, she just disappeared in a second. I will never forget that moment.

A country much bigger than Laos was conducting a secret war in our country to build a defense against our neighboring country of Vietnam. That big country was America. For nine years, bombs were dropped on my country, one bombing mission every eight minutes.

When I was thirteen and a half, the Communists took over and many of us were forced to leave because of the political turmoil. My family and friends told me I had to leave Laos. I didn't know what was going to happen and I decided to escape. Circumstances brought me to America. There I was reunited with some, but not all, of my family.

Mali and I were both the children of war. What we experienced became the energy that drew us together as friends. We are not only bound by the atrocities of our war experience, but also because living in exile inspired us to be the kind of artists we are today. We transform our life experience, our cultural heritage, to create awareness and a tool for better understanding our histories.

Stories like *Mali Under the Night Sky* are a balm that will heal the wounds of the war. Our stories can vitally inspire victims of war to face their own history and to be able to let past tragedy and trauma be resolved. I am very sure Mali's story will find its own way to inspire the hearts and souls of victims of war, of refugees, of immigrants and asylum seekers all around the world.

Thavisouk Phrasavath
Writer, artist, and filmmaker
2009 Academy Award and
Independent Spirit Award Nominee

Book and cover design by
Sergio A. Gomez

*Mali Under the Night Sky : A Lao Story of Home.* Copyright © 2010 by Youme Landowne. Illustrations copyright © 2010 by Youme Landowne.
All rights reserved. No part of this book may be used or reproduced in any manner whatsoever without written permission except in case of brief quotations for reviews. For information, write
Cinco Puntos Press, 701 Texas, El Paso, TX 79901 or call at (915) 838-1625. Printed in Hong Kong.
First Edition 10 9 8 7 6 5 4 3 2 1
Library of Congress Cataloging-in-Publication Data. Youme. Mali under the night sky : a Lao story of home / by Youme Landowne ; illustrated by Youme Landowne. — 1st ed. p. cm.
ISBN 978-1-933693-68-2 (alk. paper) 1. Kouanchao, Malichansouk, 1971–Juvenile literature. 2. Laotian American artists—Biography—Juvenile literature. I. Kouanchao, Malichansouk,
1971- II. Title. III. Title: Lao story of home. N6537.K655Y68 2010 709.2—dc22 [B] 2009042862

Thank you (khop jai)
Vannasone Keodara, Soukanh and Chomsy Kouanchao
for Lao language guidance!

Cinco Puntos Press
www.cincopuntos.com